PREPARE FOR BAPTISM

inel williams

Copyright © 2024 Inel Williams. All rights reserved.
All Bible verses are quoted from the KJV Bible.

INTRO

Baptism is a special event in the life of every Christian. It's when you are welcomed into a big family of people who all accept Jesus Christ as our Lord and Saviour.

But it is important to know: what is baptism exactly? Why do we get baptized? How does it happen spiritually and physically?

With this guide you will figure out the who, what, when, where, why and how of this important moment in your life! This will not only help you understand the ins and outs of baptism, but also give you something to look back on to remember the time when you chose to give your life to God.

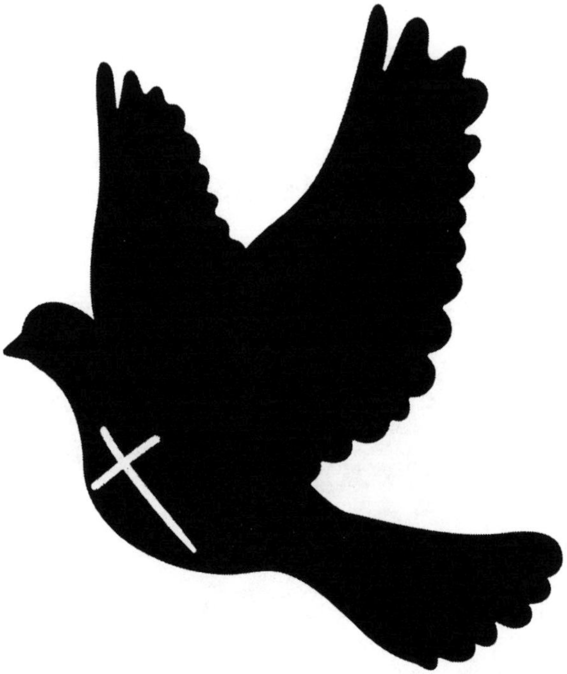

"...Repent, and be baptized every one of you in the name of Jesus Christ for the remission of sins, and ye shall receive the gift of the Holy Ghost."

ACTS 2:38-39 (KJV)

4

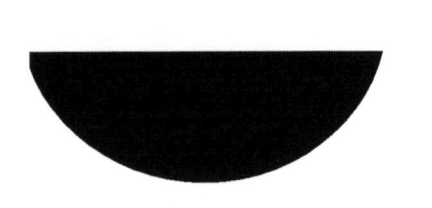

WHO

Who can be baptized? Baptism is an option for anyone who has faith in Jesus Christ. You don't have to be perfect, nor do you have to be at a certain age nor stage in life. Young or old, rich or poor, boy or girl: anyone can be baptized once they know that they trust in Jesus and want to live for Him.

Does this sound like you? If the answer is yes, then fill in the blank below:

My name is _____ , I'm a child of God, and I'm going to be baptized!

Do you know someone who is already baptized? Maybe it's your parent or guardian, your teacher, or another family member. Write down some of their names:

_____

_____

_____

_____

Let's focus on at least one of the names you wrote above. Ask this person, what do they think about baptism? How old were they when they were baptized?

_____

_____

_____

_____

_____

"Jesus answered, Verily, verily, I say unto thee, except a man be born of water and of the Spirit, he cannot enter into the kingdom of God."

JOHN 3:5

WHAT

What is baptism exactly? It is a ritual that we do to welcome new Christians. Baptism includes water: either water is sprinkled onto your forehead, or more traditionally you are <u>immersed</u> in water. To be immersed means to be completely covered by water. You experience this when you put your whole head and body underwater in a bathtub or when you're at the beach.

Baptism is a symbol of being cleansed of our old selves. In other words, baptism allows us to show on the outside how Christ has changed us on the inside. It is a public way of showing other people how we have decided to live a new life in Christ.

Baptism doesn't automatically mean that your sins are forgiven. It doesn't even mean that you are truly living for God. You have to choose to repent. You have to ask Jesus to forgive you. You should try to make an honest effort to avoid sin. Baptism doesn't mean that you will never sin again - after all, we all are sinners (Romans 3:23), but you should be more careful about your sins. What are some sins that you want to confess and forsake (stop doing)? List them below:

_____

_____

_____

_____

_____

_____

Which sin do you want to work on the most? What are at least two things you can do that will help you stop doing this sin? Avoiding this sin will make it easier to avoid other sins.

_____

_____

_____

_____

Write a brief prayer to God. Ask him to forgive you of your sins, and let him know you're ready to accept Jesus into your heart.

_____

_____

_____

_____

_____

"Therefore we are buried with him by baptism into death: that like as Christ was raised up from the dead by the glory of the Father, even so we also should walk in newness of life."

ROMANS 6:4

WHY

Why should we get baptized? There are multiple reasons, such as:
- to embrace your new identity in Christ,
- to publically show you have faith, and
- because Jesus commands it (Matt. 28:19).

Baptism is also a symbol of Jesus' death and resurrection. When you go underwater, that is like Christ dying and descending into Hell (see the Apostles' Creed on page 17). When you rise from the water, that is like Christ rising from the dead. Besides this, baptism's main goal is to show that you are now a member of the global Christian church. You declare your faith in front of others, and this helps deepen it. This follows Jesus's teaching that we should not hide our faith (Matthew 10:32-33).

Being open about declaring, sharing, and confessing your faith only strengthens it. Baptism helps you be proud of being Christian.

Imagine your life after being baptized. What do you see? Happy things? Joyful times? Will you stay the same? Will you be changed? What will your relationship with God be like? Write or draw what you see below.

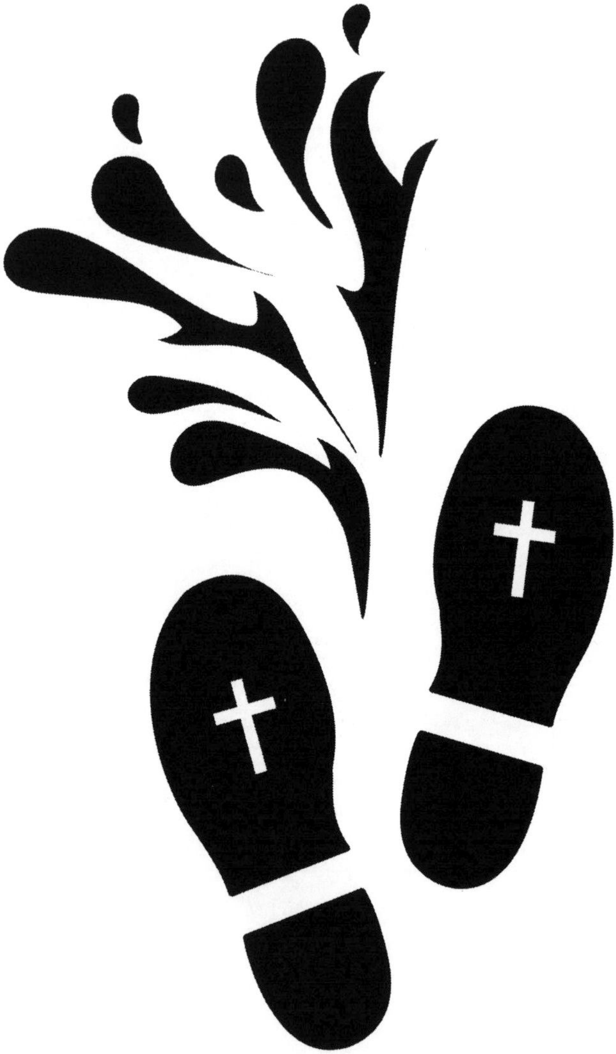

"I indeed baptize you with water unto repentance. But he that cometh after me is mightier than I, whose shoes I am not worthy to bear: he shall baptize you with the Holy Ghost, and with fire..."

MATTHEW 3:11

HOW

Upon being baptized, we receive the Holy Spirit of God. It fills, moves, and changes us in ways that only God can. It can inspire us to read the Word, share the Gospel, and be good to one another. The Holy Ghost gives us the hunger to be holy and turn away from sin. It makes us want to follow the lead of the only sinless man who has ever existed (1 Peter 2:22). You don't need to say anything during your baptism. The pastor/ priest/ elder will walk you through it. At the end he will say something like, "I now baptize you in the name of the Father, and the Son, and the Holy Spirit." To prepare further, read the creed on the next page. It is a summary of beliefs for Christians that is often used during baptisms:

THE APOSTLES' CREED

I believe in God the Father Almighty, creator of Heaven and Earth. I believe in Jesus Christ, His only Son, our Lord. He was conceived by the Holy Spirit and born of the Virgin Mary.

He suffered under Pontius Pilate, was crucified, died, and was buried. He descended into Hell. On the third day He rose again.

He ascended into Heaven, and is seated at the right hand of the Father. He will come again to judge the living and the dead.

I believe in the Holy Spirit, the holy catholic* church, the communion of saints*, the forgiveness of sins, the resurrection of the body, and the life everlasting. Amen.

*The word "catholic" means global. "Communion of saints" means all Christians, living and dead, united in Christ through baptism.

Let's answer some questions about the Apostles' Creed to remember it better.

Who was Jesus conceived by?

_____

Who did Jesus suffer under?

_____

Where is Jesus now?

_____

What will Jesus do when he comes again?

_____

What eight things do Christians believe in?

_____

_____

_____

"Let us draw near with a true heart in full assurance of faith, having our hearts sprinkled from an evil conscience, and our bodies washed with pure water."

HEBREWS 10:22

WHEN & WHERE

People are baptized in different places. This can be a church or a body of water like a river or ocean. Jesus was baptized in the Jordan River when he was about 30 (Luke 3:22-23). Where and when will you be baptized?

Date of baptism:

MON   TUE   WED   THU   FRI   SAT   SUN

___ / ___ / ___

Location of baptism:

_____

Who will bear witness
(family, friends, neighbors, etc.):

_____

_____

MY THOUGHTS & PRAYERS

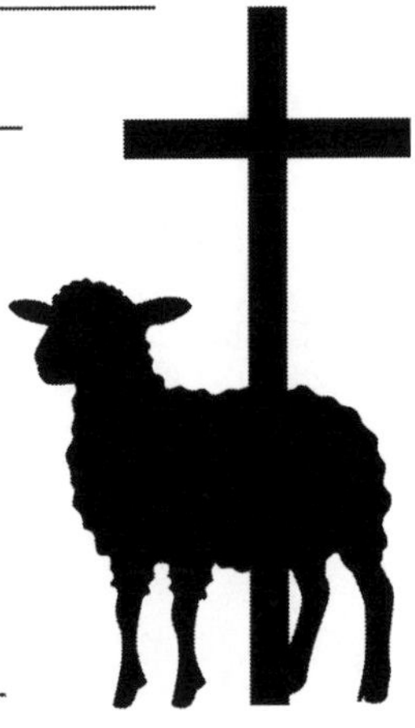

CERTIFICATE OF BAPTISM

This certifies that

_____

was officially baptized in the name of the Father, the Son, and the Holy Spirit on the _____ day of _____ at

_____

_____

by the pastor _____.

Age at baptism: _____

THOUGHTS & PRAYERS
FROM FAMILY, FRIENDS, AND LOVED ONES

A PICTURE OF MY BAPTISM

Made in the USA
Coppell, TX
18 June 2025